D0472357

THE AMAZING BOOK OF INSECT RECORDS

THE HEAVIEST, THE LOUDEST, THE MOST POISONOUS, AND MANY MORE!

BLACKBIRCH PRESS, INC.

WOODBRIDGE, CONNECTICUT

Special Thanks

The publisher would like to thank Dr. T.J. Walker, of the University of Florida, for his help and cooperation in putting this book together.

Published by Blackbirch Press, Inc.
260 Amity Road
Woodbridge, CT 06525
web site: http://www.blackbirch.com
e-mail: staff@blackbirch.com

Printed in China

10 9 8 7 6 5 4 3 2

Photo Credits
Cover and title page: ©Corel Corporation; pages 4, 8: ©PhotoDisc; pages 5–7, 9, 11, 13–15, 19, 27: ©Ed S. Ross; pages 10, 12, 16–18, 22, 24–26, 28, 30, 31: ©Corel Corporation; page 20, 21: ©J.H. Robinson/Photo Researchers, Inc.; page 23: ©LSF OSF/Animals Animals; page 29: ©George K. Bryce/Animals Animals.

Illustrations by Richard MacCabe

Library of Congress Cataloging-in-Publication Data
Woods, Samuel G.
     The amazing book of insect records: including the heaviest, the loudest, the most poisonous, and many more! / by Samuel G. Woods.
         p. cm.
     Includes bibliographical references.
     Summary: Presents information about various insects in answer to such questions as: What's the loudest insect: what's the insect that travels farthest in migration: and what's the insect with the deadliest poison?
     ISBN 1-56711-374-5
     1. Insects Miscellanea Juvenile literature. [1. Insects Miscellanea. 2. Questions and answers.] I. Title. II. Title: Insect records.
QL467.2.W64 1999   99–25283
595.7—dc21   CIP

Contents

What's the FASTEST insect?

Common horsefly

The Horsefly

This zippy kind of true fly can reach speeds of more than 90 miles per hour (145 kph)!

This horsefly is biting into human skin.

What's the LONGEST-LIVED insect?

The Wood-Boring Beetle

Certain species of this beetle can remain in a larva stage for more than 50 years!

Wood-boring beetle (adult)

Adult wood-boring beetles dig their way into wood to feed and lay eggs. The larvae often spend such a long time inside that, in the meantime, the wood is used for furniture or some other purpose. One beetle supposedly first emerged from a 40-year-old bookcase!

Wood-boring beetle (larva)

What's the insect with the DEADLIEST POISON?

The Harvester Ant

Ounce for ounce, these ants have the most toxic venom of any insect. Only 12 harvester ant stings are needed to kill a 4.4 pound (2 kilogram) rat!

These harvester ants are building a nest in the Arizona desert.

NOTEPAD

Members of the order *Hymenoptera* (ants, bees, wasps, etc.) have the most deadly poisons in the insect world. The first record of a human death resulting from an insect sting goes back to the 26th century B.C. when King Menes of Egypt was stung by a wasp or hornet.

The African Cicada

This cicada produces a calling song that has been recorded at 106.7 decibels at a distance of about 20 inches (50 centimeters). As a comparison, a jackhammer operates at about 100 decibels! (Anything over 85 decibels can be dangerous for the human ear.)

Cicada

African cicada

What's the HEAVIEST insect?

The Goliath Beetle

This behemoth beetle can weigh up to 4 ounces (100 grams), which is the weight of a quarter-pounder hamburger!

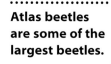

Atlas beetles are some of the largest beetles.

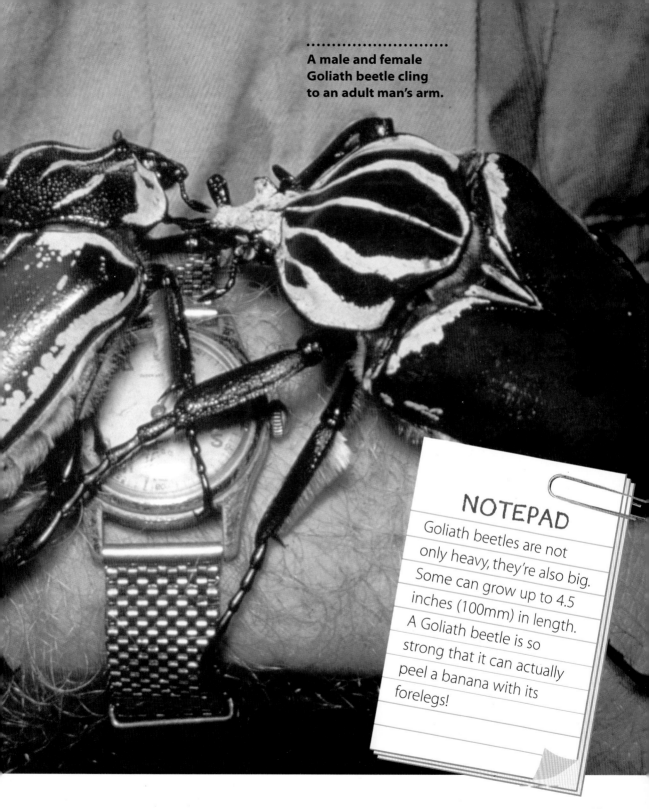

A male and female Goliath beetle cling to an adult man's arm.

NOTEPAD
Goliath beetles are not only heavy, they're also big. Some can grow up to 4.5 inches (100mm) in length. A Goliath beetle is so strong that it can actually peel a banana with its forelegs!

What's the SMALLEST insect?

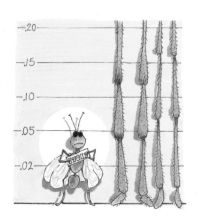

The Parasitic Wasp

One species of parasitic wasp has been recorded as the smallest overall adult insect, measuring only .05 inches (.139 centimeters). That's only a little larger than the smallest segment shown on a ruler!

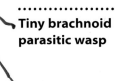

Tiny brachnoid parasitic wasp

These tiny wasps use their stingers to deposit their eggs inside the bodies or eggs of other insects. As the larvae grow, they feed on and eventually kill their host.

An adult parasitic wasp walks along the body of a caterpillar that has been host to many cocoons.

Earwigs are related to silverfish.

What's the insect with the MOST MOLTS?

The Fire Brat (also called Silverfish)

When an insect molts, it sheds its outer shell to make room for a new, larger one. Certain insects undergo many molts as they mature from larvae (developing insects) to adults. The fire brat seems to be the all-time record-holder for molts: it molts 60 times before reaching adulthood.

Common silverfish

NOTEPAD

Some fire brats can live for up to a year without food. They prefer warm temperatures and can commonly be found under rocks and bark, or in basements. They are also particularly fond of eating the glue in books!

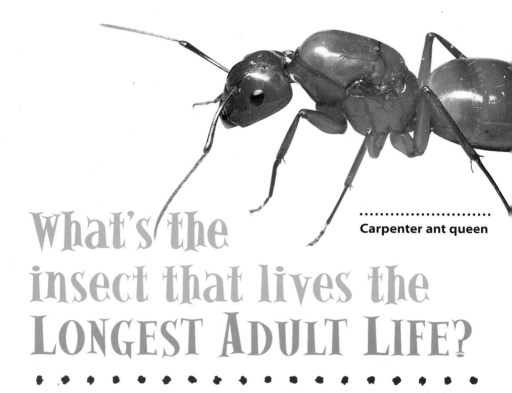

What's the insect that lives the LONGEST ADULT LIFE?

The Queen Ant

Certain queen ants have lived to be nearly 30 years old in the wild!

NOTEPAD

While worker ants in a colony live only one or two years, the queen will survive for as long as the colony does. Many colonies will last for several decades. The queen spends her entire life laying eggs.

This long-lived queen ant is a giant next to one of her worker ants.

Locust

What's the insect that TRAVELS FARTHEST in migration?

The Desert Locust

Certain kinds of locusts have been known to travel nearly 3,000 miles (4,500 kilometers). One species flew from Africa across the Atlantic Ocean to South America!

The desert locust is the insect traveling champion.

This locust is honored with another incredible insect distinction: it holds the record for the largest swarms. In Africa in 1954, a swarm of desert locusts invaded Kenya and covered an area of 77 square miles (200 square kilometers).

Scientists estimate that there were more than 50 million locusts per 1 square kilometer, making a total number of 10 billion locusts in one swarm!

What's the insect with the FASTEST WING BEAT?

The Midge

This tiny, fly-like creature can beat its wings at a frequency of 1046 hertz—that means more than 1,000 times per second! By comparison, a common housefly beats its wings only about 180 times per second.

Midges look like
miniature flies.

A swarm of tiny midges
moves through the air.

NOTEPAD

These blood-sucking insects are small enough to get through human clothing. They are most often found near streams and ponds, which is where their larvae develop. Young midges actually live underwater for the first part of their lives.

Scavenger ants are some of the few animals that can survive the harsh environment of the Sahara Desert.

What's the insect that can withstand the MOST HEAT?

The Scavenger Ant

Desert-dwelling scavenger ants can be found in the Sahara Desert of Africa, as well as in North American deserts in the southwest. Some species have been known to go out hunting in temperatures above 140 degrees Fahrenheit (60 degrees C)!

A scavenger ant colony tends to its newly hatched larvae.

What's the insect that gives off the BRIGHTEST LIGHT?

The Jamaican Click Beetle

The light flashes of this very large beetle species have been recorded as the brightest of all insects. By comparison, the click beetle's light is thought to be about 10 times brighter than that of a common firefly (which is not really a fly— it's another kind of beetle).

Click beetle

The Jamaican click beetle is also called the eyed click beetle.

Atlas moth
caterpillar

What's the insect with the LARGEST WINGS?

The Atlas Moth

In terms of overall wing surface area, this huge Asian moth holds the record. With wings that can extend more than 9 or 10 inches (23–25 centimeters), some atlas moths have a wing surface area of roughly 16 to 17 square inches (12 square centimeters) per wing!

The atlas moth—shown nearly actual size—is a giant in the world of flying insects.

Glossary

Behemoth—something of monstrous size and power.

Bioluminescence—the emission of light from living organisms.

Colony—a large group of insects that live and work together.

Decibel—unit for measuring the volume of sounds.

Hertz—unit for measuring the frequency of vibrations and waves, equal to one cycle per second.

Host—an animal or plant from which a parasite gets nutrition.

Larva—an insect in the stage of development between egg and adult, when it looks like a worm.

Migration—when animals or insects go to live in another region or climate at a certain time of the year or point in their lives.

Molt—to shed an outer covering so a new one can grow.

Protein—a nourishing substance found in all plant and animal cells.

Species—one of the groups into which animals are divided according to their shared characteristics.

Thorax—the part of an insect's body between its head and its abdomen.

Venom—poison produced by some insects.

For More Information

Books

Anderson, Margaret Jean. *Bizarre Insects*. Springfield, NJ: Enslow Publishers, Inc., 1996.

Parker, Steve. Ann Salvage (Illustrator). *Beastly Bugs* (Creepy Creatures). Chatham, NY: Raintree Steck Vaughn, 1993.

Wechsler, Doug. *Bizarre Bugs*. New York, NY: Cobblehill, 1995.

Videos

James Earl Jones. *Insects: The Little Things That Run the World* (1989).

Web Sites

Fun Insect Facts
Uncover strange facts about well-known insects—ham.spu.umn.edu/kris/science.html.

Get This Bug Off Me!
Broaden your understanding of the insect world by learning which bugs are dangerous and which are harmless—www.uky.edu/Agriculture/Entomology/ythfacts/hurtrnot.htm.

Index